INTRODUCTION

My Love for Motorcycles started you could say at 5 years old. I played and played with the Auburn toy rubber Motorcycles. I had then 7 or 8 of the Rubber Motorcycles. That's when I started riding Motorcycles, all my older brothers had them. Brother Al's Moped is what I rode first. At the age of 9, I was riding Brother Denny's 250 Harley Sprint up hills.

Then in 1980 I ran with the Joey Chitwood Thrill Show and did the M̶ Firewall Stunt. After the season with Joey's Show ᴐ ˙ very dangerous and difficult Firewall Stunt. I contacted That's Incredible and started working on the project, also at the same time was busy driving truck. Well finally after 2 years all said and done, I did that Incredible Stunt. The Firewall Stunt on the back cover is the simple Motorcycle Firewall Stunt I did with the Joey Chitwood Thrill Show.

Then after moving back to Minnesota, I did some Motorcycle Jumps in my area. I would Jump my Motorcycle off ramp lengthwise over my Cadillac & trailer unto the ground. Decided to hang my shoes up from Jumping because it was getting hard to find ramp hands to help set-up. But I still get the urge now & then.

Planning on doing a Record Jump someday when I get older. To be the oldest to do a Motorcycle Jump. Which I'm not sure how old that is. Meanwhile after 12 years of collecting and counting, I'm having fun in the Toy Business.

ISBN 0-9652650-0-5
Library of Congress No. 96-94423
Printed in the United States of America

Author, Photographer, & Publisher
Scott Johnson
RR 1 Box 74
Leroy, Mn. 55951
(507) 324-5772

The prices in this book should be used only as a guide. As in one part of the Country may differ from another. The Author assumes no responsibility for losses that could occur in using this guide.

August, 1996

Grading Guide

In this book I have grades for Good, Excellent, and Mint condition. This guide is for complete and original toys. Some pictures show boxes that came with toy, but prices don't include box. See Guide on Boxes.

The following Grades hold true except grading Cast-Iron.

GOOD – Complete, original, well worn, scratched, small dents, minor rust, or warage.

EXCELLENT – Minor scratches, no dents or rust, minor wear, light fading.

MINT – Like new condition.

Cast-Iron Grading

GOOD – Little or no paint, but original and complete with riders. Some rust, minor cracks.

EXCELLENT – 60 to 70% of paint intact, minor rust, no cracks.

MINT – Like new condition.

If a cast-iron piece has been repainted, 95% of the time it's probably been repaired. A repainted or repaired piece is valued at 60 to 75% of Good condition price. If it's an old repaint it's value is good condition value. Be careful in knowing the difference between an original and reproduction one, as some people are making these. It helps to know the history if ones not sure.

Cast-Iron Value for Separate Riders

Original Hubley Cop Driver – $200-$350
Original Hubley Cop rider in side car – $200-$350

Original Civilian Hubley Driver – $350-$650
Original Civilian Hubley Lady in side car – $350-$650

Original Large Hubley Popeye – $600-$1200
Original Small Hubley Popeye – $400-$650

Original Vindex Cop – $400-$700
Original Vindex cop rider in side car – $400-$700

       All the Above riders have been reproduced
All reproduced Drivers and Riders (except large Popeye) – $50-$75
Reproduced large Popeye – $75-$125

Box Value Guide

Grading the value of a box depends on Condition, Demand, and Rarity. The value of a box is one of the percentages below of that Toy in mint condition.

1) 20% to 35% – Most boxes fall in this category, more attainable.
2) 35% to 60% – Boxes that are hard to find, and/or more in demand.
3) 60% to 100% – Boxes that are rare and/or very much sought after.

Table of Contents

Dedication:

In memory of my Dad, Emmett Johnson
who died of cancer at age 71.

Special Thanks:

Nancy, Marian, Henry, Jerry,
Gary, Mark, Zack & Hiliary

Rubber Motorcyles

Cop Cycles, 3¾", with spokes, Auburn, USA C. 1958-1963
20-30-40

Cop Cycle, 3¾", no spokes, Auburn, USA C. 1953-1958
25-35-45

Cop Cycle, 3¾", Pink Auburn, USA C. 1950's
30-40-50

Scout with gunner, 3¼", Auburn, USA C. 1941
50-100-150

Motorcycle Scout, 3¾", Auburn, USA C. 1941
50-100-150

Rubber Motorcyles

Motorcycle Cops, 5",
Auburn, USA C. 1940
60-120-200

Motorcycle Cop, 4",
Auburn, USA C. 1940
45-90-150

Servicar, 4¼",
Auburn, USA C. 1958
50-100-150

Rubber Motorcyles

Motorcycle Cops, 6¼",
Auburn, USA C. 1950's
50-100-150

Cycles, 5", vinyl, Hong
Kong C. Early 1970's
10-15-20

Motorcyle Cop, 6¼",Auburn,
Later Vinyl, USA C. Late 1960's
25-50-75

Plastic Motorcyles

Honda Cycle, 6½",
Gay Toys, USA C. 1965
50-75-100

Gay Police, 7½",
Gay Plastic, USA
C. Mid 1960's
20-30-40

Motorcycle Cop, 9",
Probably Renwal,
USA C. 1960's
40-65-100

Plastic Motorcycles

Motorcycle & sidecar, 5",
Renwal, USA C. 1950's
85-125-175

Motorcyle Cop, 3¾",
Renwal, USA C. 1953
65-100-150

Military Cycle, 3½", Thomas Toys, USA C. 1950's
75-125-175

Plastic Motorcycles

Service-car, 4½",
Thomas Toys,
USA C. 1950's
125-175-250

Motorcycle Riders, 3½",
Thomas Toys & ACME,
USA C. 1950's
without riders 50-80-115
with riders   60-90-125

Cycle & sidecar with
girl, 3¾", Thomas Toys,
USA C. 1950's
150-225-300

Plastic Motorcycles

Vespa Scooter, 4",
Thomas Toys, USA
C. 1955
35-65-100

Motorcycle, 5", wind-up,
Precision Plastics,
USA C. 1950's
60-90-125

Cop Cycle, 4", wind-up,
USA C. 1950's
75-100-125

Plastic Motorcycles

Police Servicar, 4¾",
wind-up, Lincoln,
USA C. 1950's
100-175-250

Motorcycle & Sidecar, 5½",
Friction, Nosco Plastics,
USA C. 1950's
150-250-400

Cop N Car, 8½" & 4", motor &
siren, Automatic Toy Co.,
USA C. 1953
100-175-250

Plastic Motorcycles

Traffic Cop Set, 1⅞" & 4",
Revell, USA C. 1950's
bike alone 10-15-20
set   20-35-50

Fix-All Motorcycle, 12",
B/O, Marx, USA C. 1950's
200-325-500

Tom & Jerry Scooter,
4½", Friction, Marx,
Hong Kong C. 1973
50-75-100

Plastic Motorcycles

Motorcycle Combo, 4",
Friction, Hong Kong
C. Late 1960's
25-50-75

Race Cycle, 3¾", Friction,
Plastic shell covering tin
litho. Japan C. 1960's
30-45-60

Cop Whistles, 4", Common-
wealth, USA C. 1950's
25-40-60

Plastic Motorcycles

Cop Whistle, 3½", Gerber,
USA C. Early 1950's
35-50-75

Motorcycle Cop & sidecar,
6⅜", wind-up Ideal,
USA C. 1950
200-325-500

Rocket Cycle, 6½",
Ideal, USA C. 1950's
200-300-400

Plastic Motorcycles

Military Cycle & side-
car, 3⅜", Pyro, USA
C. Early 1950's
60-90-125

Cycle & sidecar with
baby, 3⅜", Pyro,
USA C. 1950's
75-125-175

Cop Cycles, 5", Hubley,
USA C. 1950's
50-100-150

Police Cycle, 8¾", Friction with moving pistons, Japan C. Early 1960's
225-350-500

Same bike above but no Foot Rests
200-300-450

Harley Davidson, 9", Friction with moving pistons, Japan C. Early 1960's
300-450-650

Harley Davidson Motorcycle, 9", Friction, TN, Japan C. Late 1950's
350-500-750

Meguro 170, 11¾", Friction, Bandai, Japan C. 1950's
1000-1600-2500

Venus Motorcycle, 9", Friction, TN, Japan C. 1960
250-400-600

Civilian Motorcycles, Tin

Comet Cycle, 9", Friction,
N, Japan C. 1960's
250-500-750

Hunter, 6¾", Friction,
TN, Japan C. 1950's
225-400-600

Motorcyclist, 3¼", Friction,
LineMar, Japan C. 1960's
50-100-150

Civilian Motorcycles, Tin

Motorcycle Girl, 8",
Friction, Haji,
Japan C. 1960's
175-275-400

Indian, 3⅝", Friction,
Japan C. 1950's
100-175-250

General Motorcycle, 8½",
Friction, MT, Japan C. 1960
300-550-850

Civilian Motorcycles, Tin

Flip-over Motorcycle, 5¾",
wind-up, Japan C. 1940
150-250-400

Flip-over Motorcycle, 5¾",
Friction, Alps, Japan C. 1960's
125-175-250

Motorcyclist, 7", wind-up,
TCO, Germany C. 1950's
500-850-1300

Civilian Motorcycles, Tin

Mac 700, 7½", wind-up, Arnold, US. Zone Germany C. 1950's
350-600-900

Cycle & Sidecar, 8", wind-up, Tipp, Germany C. Later 1930's
400-650-1000

Civilian Motorcycles, Tin

Atom Cycle, 11¾", B/O, MT, Japan C. 1960
350-600-900

World Champion, 11¾", B/O, MT, Japan C. 1950's
375-675-1000

Civilian Motorcycles, Tin

Condor Motorcycle, 11¾", Friction, IY. Metal Toys, Japan C. 1950's
1000-1600-2500

Harley Davidson, 16", Friction, IY. Metal Toys, Japan C. 1950's
2250-5000-8000

Race Motorcycles, Tin

Comet Racer, No. 48, 4⅜", Friction,
Japan C. Late 1950's
125-200-300

Magic Motor Cycle Top, 4" dia., wind-up, Line Mar,
Japan C. 1950's
200-325-500

Race cycle No. 18, 3½", Friction,
Japan C. Mid 1960's
20-30-40

Race Cycle No. 25, 3¾", wind-up, Stone,
Japan C. 1960's
100-150-200

Race Cycle No. 27, 3½", Friction,
Japan C. 1960's
50-100-150

Crown Auto Cycle No. 3, 3½", Friction, Alps,
Japan C. 1950's
85-135-185

Race Motorcycles, Tin

Race Cycle, No. 12, 5¼", wind-up,
US.Zone Germany C. 1940's
125-200-300

Race Cycle, 5¾", wind-up, Kellerman,
Germany C. Late 1940's
275-550-850

Race Cycle, 3¾", Fits on a rod to a w/u box. Freewheeling,
US.Zone Germany, C. Late 1940's
50-75-125

Race Cycle No. 25, 3½", wind-up, Huki,
Germany C. 1950's
100-150-200

Schuco, Curvo 1000, 4¾", wind-up,
Germany C. 1950's
200-325-550

Race cycle, 5¼", wind-up, Schuco, US.Zone Germany,
C. Late 1940's Early 1950's
175-300-500

Race Motorcycles, Tin

Race Cycle No. 60, 7¾",
Friction, TN, Japan C. 1960's
125-225-350

Race Cycle, 8", Friction,
Asahi, Japan C. 1960's
125-225-350

Harley Cycle No. 7, 5½",
Friction, Japan C. 1960's
75-125-200

Race Motorcycles, Tin

Race Cycle No. 4, 7",
wind-up, Technofix,
U.S. Zone, Germany C. 1950's
150-250-375

Race Cycle No. 2, 7", wind-up,
Technofix, France C. 1960's
125-225-350

Race Cycle No. 15, 7", wind-up,
Technofix, Germany C. 1940
175-300-450

Race Cycle, 5¼", Occupied
Japan C. 1940's
200-300-400

Race Cycle No. 30, 8",
Friction, TN, Japan C. 1960's
150-250-375

Mechanical Motor Cycle
No. 25, 8", wind-up, Y, Japan
C. Late 1960's
75-125-175

Race Motorcycles, Tin

Race Cycle, 7¼", wind-up, Huki, Germany C. 1956
250-450-750

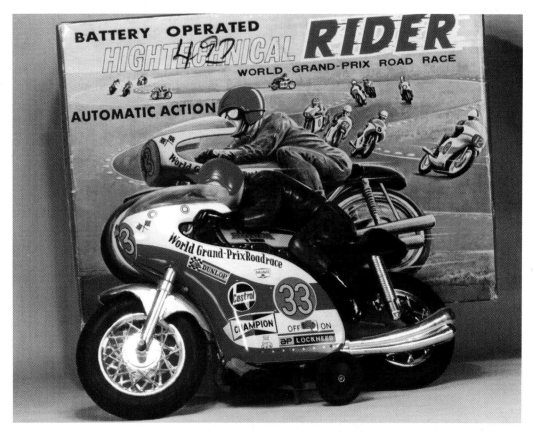

Grand-Prix Race Cycle No. 33, 10", B/O, TPS, Japan C. 1960's
100-200-300

Clowns & Animals, Tin

Clown Cycle, 6¼", Friction,
Japan C. 1950's
250-450-700

Monkey Cycle, 5", wind-up,
Bandai, Japan C. 1960's
125-200-300

Clown Cycle, 6¼", wind-up,
Japan C. 1950's
250-450-700

Clowns & Animals, Tin

Monkey Cycle, 5⅜", Friction,
This ones missing umbrella.
Japan C. 1950
275-500-750

Animal Cycle, 5¼", Friction,
Haji, Japan C. 1960's
65-90-125

Clown Cycle, 7½", wind-up,
Mettoy, England C. 1950's
450-850-1250

Wall of Death Circus Bear,
6" dia., wind-up,
Japan C. 1960's
125-200-300

Monkey Cycle, 9¾", Friction,
ATC, Japan C. 1950
200-325-500

Acrobatic Monkeys, 10½", dia.,
wind-up, Wyandotte,
USA C. 1930's
250-450-700

Military Motorcycles, Tin

Combat Cycle, 7¾", Friction, Japan C. 1950's
250-450-700

Police Auto Cycle, 11¾", B/O, Bandai, Japan C. 1950's
175-300-450

Military Motorcycles, Tin

Military Rider, 7½", wind-up, Arnold, US. Zone Germany C. Late 1940's
250-450-700

Military Cop with gun, 8¼", wind-up, Marx, USA C. 1930's
300-500-750

Military Rider, 7½", wind-up, Arnold, Germany C. 1950's
275-500-750

Motorcycle Scout, 7½", wind-up, Arnold, Germany C. 1935
350-700-1100

Military Motorcycles, Tin

U.S. Army Motorcycle, 8",
Friction, TN, Japan C. 1960's
175-275-400

Military Cycle & side car, 4",
wind-up, France C. 1950's
75-150-250

Military Police, 5¼", wind-up,
K, Japan C. Late 1940's
200-300-425

Military Motorcycles, Tin

Military Cycle & Sidecar,
4", SFA. France C. 1935
100-200-300

Military Police, 3½", Friction,
Japan C. Mid 1960's
15-25-35

MP Cycle, 6¾", Friction,
MT., Japan C. 1950's
200-375-550

Military Motorcycles, Tin

Navy Cycle, 5½", Friction,
Japan C. 1960's
50-100-150

PD Cycle, 5½", Friction,
TYO, Japan C. 1950's
150-250-350

Military Cycle, 5½", wind-up,
KT, Japan C. Late 1940's
250-425-650

Police Motorcycles, Tin

PD. Cycle, 7", Friction,
TYO, Japan C. 1950's
225-400-600

Police Motorcycle & Sidecar,
6¾", Friction, MT, Japan C. 1950's
400-700-1100

Police Cycle, 7¾", Friction,
Y, Japan C. 1950's
250-450-700

Police Motorcycles, Tin

Police Motorcycle, 8⅜", wind-up, Marx, USA C. 1930's
300-500-750

Motorcycle Cop, 8⅛", wind-up, Marx, USA C. 1950's
200-325-450

Police Cycle & side car, 8¼", wind-up, Marx, USA C. 1930's
300-500-750

Police Motorcycles, Tin

Daredevil Motorcycle Cop,
8⅜", wind-up, Unique Art,
USA C. 1935
300-500-750

Police Cycle, 8", Friction,
HAJI, Japan C. Mid 1960's
75-125-175

Police Cycle, 7", wind-up,
K., Japan C. 1950's
300-500-750

Police Motorcycles, Tin

Police Cycle, 5½", Friction,
Hadson, Japan C. 1950's
200-325-475

Police Cycle, 7¼", wind-up,
LineMar, Japan C. 1950's
250-375-550

Pinched, 10" square, wind-up,
Marx, USA C. 1927
300-600-900

Police Motorcycles, Tin

Police Cycle & Car, 7" & 3¾",
Friction car, Freewheeling
cycle. TKK., Japan C. Early 1960's
150-250-375

Patrol Cycle, 8", Friction,
Japan C. 1950's
150-250-375

PD Indian Cycle, 8½", Friction,
MT, Japan C. Late 1950's
Missing headlight, bars &
arms not original.
450-750-1100

Patrol Auto-Tricycle, 10", B/O, TN, Japan C. Mid 1960's
100-200-300

Patrol Auto-Tricycle, 10", B/O, TN., Japan C. Late 1950's
150-250-375

Police Motorcycles, Tin

Police Cycle, 11¾", B/O, MT, Japan C. 1950's
325-550-800

Highway Patrol, 8", Friction, Asahi, Japan C. 1960's
175-275-400

Police Motorcycles, Tin

Police Cycle, 11¼", B/O, Tipp., West Germany C. 1950's
900-1500-2250

Highway Patrol & sidecar, 10¼", Friction, ATC, Japan C. Early 1960's
375-650-950

Highway PD., 10½", Friction, ATC, Japan C. Late 1950's
200-300-450

Motorcycle Cop, 10½", B/O, Daiya, Japan C. 1950's
400-750-1250

G. Men Cycle, 10", Friction, Hadson, Japan C. 1950's
750-1250-1850

Siren Patrol Motorcycle, 11¾", B/O, MT, Japan C. Mid 1960's
325-550-800

Police Motorcycles, Tin

Mystic Motorcycle, 4½", wind-up, Marx,
USA C. Late 1930's
75-150-225

Police Cycle & side car, 4½", Friction,
Y, Japan C. 1950's
250-350-500

Tricky Motorcycle, 4¼", wind-up, Marx,
USA C. 1930's
125-200-300

Motorcycle Cable Rider, 4¾", wind-up,
Asahi, Japan C. 1950's
150-225-350

Police Cycle, 3⅝", Freewheeling, missing Friction pull car.
Japan C. 1950's Bike alone
50-75-125

Motorcycle Cop & Car, 5¾", & 3½", wind-up,
DBP, West Germany C. 1950's
300-500-750

Police Dept. Trike, 6½",
wind-up, KO, Japan C. 1960's
175-275-400

Delivery Trike, 6½", wind-up,
KO, Japan C. 1960's
200-300-425

Police Dept. Trike, 6½",
wind-up, KO, Japan C. 1960's
175-275-400

Scooters & Trikes, Tin

Jantzen Bathing Suit Girl, 6½",
wind-up, Buffalo Toys,
USA C. 1930's
300-500-750

Vespa, 8½", Friction, Bandai,
Japan C. 1960
300-600-950

Servicycle, 7", wind-up,
Ny-Lint, USA C. 1948
225-400-600

Zundapp Scooter, 7", Friction,
DBGM. West Germany
C. 1950's
250-500-750

Rabbit Scooter, 6½", Friction,
Japan C. 1950's
400-700-1050

Ice Cream Scooter, 6½",
wind-up, Courtland,
USA C. 1950
100-150-225

Scooters & Trikes, Tin

Speed Boy, 9", wind-up, Marx, USA C. 1930's
275-400-600

Speed Boy, 9", wind-up & B/O lights. Marx, USA C. 1930's
300-450-650

Speed Boy, 9", wind-up, Marx, USA C. 1930's
250-375-550

Speed Boy, 9", wind-up, Marx, USA C. Late 1930's
250-375-550

Scooters & Trikes, Tin

Side Car, 10", B/O, SAN, Japan C. 1950's
900-1500-2250

Cycle-Car, 10½", wind-up, Hoge, USA C. Late 1920's
2000-4500-7000+

Silver Pigeon, 9", Friction, Bandai, Japan C. 1950's
500-850-1300

King Scooter, 9¼", Friction, Y, Japan C. 1950's
650-1150-1750

Die-cast & Lead Motorcycles

Military Cycle, 2¾", Manoil, USA C. 1950's
20-35-50

Military Cycle, 3¼", Manoil, USA C. 1939
25-50-75

Motorcycle, 3", Unknown C. 1950's
20-35-50

Motorcycle Scout, 3½", Barclay, USA C. 1950's
50-85-125

Cycle, 3½", Unknown C. 1950's
20-35-50

BMW Cycle, 4¼", Unknown C. 1950's
35-65-100

Die-cast & Lead Motorcycles

Cycle & sidecar, 2½",
Barclay, USA C. 1930's
50-75-125

Cop Cycle, 8½", Hubley,
USA C. 1950's
350-650-1000

Parcel Delivery, 3½",
Barclay, USA C. 1931
75-130-200

Die-cast & Lead Motorcycles

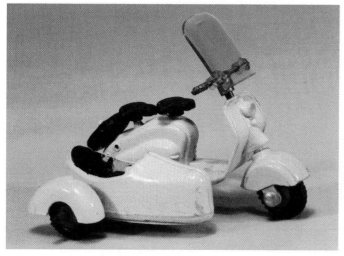

Lambretta Scooter, 2½", Unknown C. 1960's
20-35-50

Lambretta Scooter, 2", Matchbox, England C. 1960
25-50-75

Delivery Motorcycle, 3", Tootsietoy, USA C. 1933
175-275-400

Harley & sidecar, 2½", Matchbox, England C. 1963
50-85-125

Sunbeam Motorcycle, 2¾", Matchbox, England C. 1962
25-50-75

Triumph with sidecar, 2", Matchbox, England C. 1959
50-75-100

Die-cast & Lead Motorcycles

Military Cycle, 3¼", England C. 1950's
20-35-50

Motorcycle Scout, 2½", Britains, England C. 1960's
35-60-90

Military Cycles, 2⅞", Britains, England C. 1950's
20-35-50

Military Cycle, 3¼", France C. 1930's
25-50-75

Scooter, 1¾", Tootsietoy, USA C. 1960's
5-10-15

Thundercycle, 5¼", Metal & Plastic, slot-racer
Aurora, USA C. 1966
25-50-75

Die-cast & Lead Motorcycles

Dinky Cycles, 1¾", England C. pre & post-war
pre - 60-100-150
post - 40-65-100

Indian, 3", Tekno, Denmark C. 1950's
50-75-100

Cracker Jack Cycles, 1⅜", USA C. 1950's
20-35-50

Misc. Motorcycles, 1¼" to 2", Unknown, 1950's
each - 10-20-35

Triumph, 2½", Britains, England C. 1950's
50-75-100

BMW, 2½", Britains, England C. 1950's
50-75-100

Cast-Iron Motorcycles

Scooter, 4⅛", AC. Williams,
USA C. Late 1930's
275-450-650

Motorcycle Cop, 4¾", AC.
Williams, USA C. 1930's
rarer green
150-300-500

Motorcycle Cops, 4¾", AC.
Williams, USA C. 1930's
150-275-450

Cast-Iron Motorcycles

Cop Cycle, 7", A.C. Williams,
USA C. 1930's rarer green
350-650-950

Patrol, 6¼", USA C. 1930's
250-400-600

Motorcycle Cop, 7",
A.C. Williams, USA C. 1930's
350-600-900

Cast-Iron Motorcycles

Cop & sidecar, 4", Champion,
USA C. 1930's
200-325-500

Motorcycle Cop, 4¾",
Champion, USA C. 1930's
125-250-400

Motorcycle Cop & sidecar, 5",
Champion, USA C. 1930's
275-450-700

Cast-Iron Motorcycles

Motorcycle Cop, 7", Champion,
USA C. 1930's
300-500-750

Cop & Sidecar, 6", Champion,
USA C. 1930's
350-600-900

Special Delivery, 4¼", Kilgore,
USA C. 1930's
325-550-850

Cast-Iron Motorcycles

Delivery Motorcycle, 4",
Kilgore, USA C. 1930's
225-375-550

Civilian Motorcycle, 5¾",
Kilgore, USA C. 1930's
400-650-900

Motorcycles, 4⅛", Kilgore,
USA C. 1930's
125-225-350

Cast-Iron Motorcycles

Cop Cycles, 3", Hubley,
USA C. 1930's
75-135-200

Motorcycle & sidecar, 5",
Kilgore, USA. 1930's
250-400-600

Cop Cycle, Harley Davidson,
7", Swivel head, Hubley,
USA C. 1933
450-800-1300

Cast-Iron Motorcycles

Motorcycle Cop & sidecar, 4",
Hubley, USA C. 1930's
125-185-275

Civilian Harley Davidson, 6¼",
Hubley, USA C. 1930's
250-500-750

Cop Cycles, 4⅛", Hubley,
USA C. 1930's
85-150-225

Cast-Iron Motorcycles

Motorcycle Cop, 8½",
Hubley, USA C. 1930's
750-1300-2000

Motorcycle Cop &
Sidecar, 8½", Hubley,
USA C. 1930's
1000-1750-2750

Motorcycle Cop, 8¾",
Hubley, USA C. 1930's
1000-1750-3000

Cast-Iron Motorcycles

Cop Cycle, 5½", Harley Jr.,
Hubley, USA C. 1930's
300-500-750

Cop Cycles, 5½",
Hubley, USA
C. 1930's
250-450-700

Motorcycle & sidecar,
5¼", Fake rider,
Hubley, USA C. 1930's
350-700-1000

Cast-Iron Motorcycles

Motorcycle Cop &
Sidecar, 8¾", Hubley,
USA C. 1930's
1500-2500-3750

Indian 4-cyl., 9¼",
Hubley, USA C. 1929
2000-3500-5500

Motorcycle Cop, 8½",
B/O, Hubley, USA
C. 1931
1500-2500-4000

Cast-Iron Motorcycles

Cop, 4", Hubley,
USA C. 1930's
100-175-275

Indian Crash Car,
6½", Hubley, USA
C. 1930's
375-700-1000

PDH Tandem, 4⅛",
Hubley, USA C. 1930's
150-250-350

Cast-Iron Motorcycles

Traffic car, 3¼",
Hubley, USA C. 1930's
200-350-550

Crash Cars, 4⅝",
Hubley, USA C.
1930's
125-185-275

Traffic car, 4½",
Hubley, USA
C. 1930's
200-325-500

Cast-Iron Motorcycles

Cop Cycle, 7", Harley,
Swivel head, Hubley,
USA C. 1932
500-900-1400

Cop Cycle, 4¼",
Hubley, USA
C. 1930's
125-175-250

Motorcycle Cop, 6¼",
B/O, Hubley, USA
C. 1930's
275-500-750

Cast-Iron Motorcycles

Speed cycle, 4¼",
Hubley, USA C.
1933
200-350-500

Flowers, 4⅜", Hubley,
USA C. 1930's
850-1350-2000

They made 6 different
sizes of the Flowers
Cycles. They were all
blue, except size 9½"
which also was red.

Size 10¾", Large one
8000-12000-20000

Popeye Spinach Patrol,
5¼", Hubley, USA
C. 1938
650-1200-1800

Cast-Iron Motorcycles

Civilian Cycle &
sidecar, 6¼",
Hubley, USA
C. 1930's
500-1000-1500

Race Cycles, 5¾",
Hubley, USA
C. 1930's
275-500-750

Armored Motorcycle,
8¾", Hubley, USA
C. 1928
1750-2750-4500

Cast-Iron Motorcycles

Parcel Post, 9¾", Hubley, USA C. 1928
1750-3000-5000

Traffic Car, 11½", Hubley, USA C. 1930
2750-4500-7000+

Cast-Iron Motorcycles

Speed Cop & sidecar,
8½", Vindex, USA
C. 1928-1929
3250-5000-8000+

Speed Cop, 8½",
Vindex, USA
C. 1928-1929
2750-4500-7000+

PDQ Delivery, 8¾",
Vindex, USA
C. 1928-1929
4000-6500-10000+